M000011331

Baked Ombré Stained Glass, page 5

Rose Topiary, page 8

It's a Hoot Magazine Box, page 11

Photo Cube, page 14

Gadget Charging Station, page 17

Antique Photo Tile, page 19

Wiggly Wall Art, page 22

Little Rembrandt Art Storage Box, page 25

Surf & Sand Bracelet, page 28

Child's Artwork Necklace, page 30

Fabric Mosaic Table, page 32

Damask Dresser, page 34

Family Photo Canvases, page 37

Mod Podge

Does the name call to mind heavily shellacked Volkswagen Beetles?

If so, you must be a hardcore podger. Mod Podge's® roots date back to the 1960s when decoupage was all the rage. It was used to decoupage nearly everything in its early years—from wall-art collages to chairs to cars. It was popular then because of its versatility and ease of use, which of course, still rings true.

But what the modern podger understands is that Mod Podge is so much more than that. There is an expansive line of products inspired by the original recipe. You can get specialty Podge for an impressive array of endeavors—brushstroke podge that makes your photos look like paintings, antique podge that makes your crafts and photos look antique, outdoor podge which is weather resistant, podge Wash Out—(the even safer version of Mod Podge for kids) which is completely washable from all surfaces, even clothes!—Dimensional Magic, an enamel-type substance which dries hard, glossy and puffy and Photo Transfer Medium, to name just a few. But what really makes Mod Podge more than simply a decoupage medium is creativity. Thinking outside the box and applying Mod Podge to new things in new ways. And really, the sky is the limit.

I grew up in an environment that fostered and encouraged creative thinking and hands-on experimentation. With my mom and sister in the lead, I engaged in crafts of all types, and podge was no exception. Clearly, my younger self thought of Mod Podge as a very thorough and more-than-sufficient adhesive. As I've grown and matured, I've broadened my crafting horizons, and I believe Mod Podge has too. I'd like to present this book as a "Modern" Decoupage or MOD Mod Podge. In other words, this is not your mama's podge!

About the Author

Kimberly is a full-time mommy to a wise little 4-year-old (going on 20) and a very busy 2-year-old and a weekday caregiver to her sweet and sassy 4-year-old niece. Her job as professional wife and mom allows her much creative freedom which she enjoys exploring with her kids. In a former life, she was a theatre performance major and English literature minor and still enjoys plays and musicals of all types. Some of her favorite authors include Shakespeare, Oscar Wilde, Virginia Woolf and Sylvia Plath, with some Orson Scott Card and Brandon Sanderson thrown in. She's incredibly lucky to be married to her best friend.

Kimberly is an avid crafter and particularly enjoys creating with Mod Podge, hot glue, spray paint and upcycled/recycled mediums of all kinds. She currently dabbles in baking and cooking, sewing (especially for her children) and photography. She is passionate about writing, lifelong learning, her family and the color yellow. In her (admittedly limited) free time, when she is not creating, she enjoys reading, talking, singing loudly to the likes of Mumford and Sons, Adele and Mindy Gledhill, and blogging. You can find a chronicle of her creative endeavors on her blog: bugaboo, mini, mr & me (http://bugaboominimrme.blogspot.com).

General Instructions

Brayer

A brayer is a podger's best friend. This tool is the best way to eliminate air bubbles that pop up. And no matter how hard you try to keep them at bay, they will pop up.

There are many different kinds of brayers, from plain-Jane, basic brayers to blinged-out, top-of-the-line brayers. You don't need to spend a fortune on a brayer. You do need to pick a brayer that is right for you.

- Make sure it is suitable in size for the projects you're completing. Will you need to squeeze it into tight spaces? Cover a lot of ground?
- Pay attention to comfort. Will you be using it a lot or for long periods? Or is it just for the occasional podge project?
- It has got to be easy to clean. Will the roller pop off? Can it be washed with normal soap and water?

Squeegee

Why do you need a squeegee? For the same reason you need a brayer—air bubbles! It also helps smooth down the paper or fabric.

A purchased rubber or silicone craft squeegee with angled edges is recommended. The silicone is nice because it washes easily and the angled edges produce a nice result.

In a pinch, an old laminated card, such as a library card, does the trick but is prone to leaving marks or tearing paper if you aren't careful.

Fingers

More often than not I find that my fingers really are the best tool when it comes to podging! They are easily accessible, instinctually manipulated, pretty dexterous—most of the time—and easy to clean.

Brushes

I find foam brushes work best to apply the Mod Podge. They are reusable, but also incredibly affordable, which makes them somewhat disposable for those times when you forget to wash them out. Foam brushes don't leave brushstrokes, which for most projects is a plus.

If you use regular artist's paintbrushes to apply Mod Podge, be aware that they will leave visible strokes and may shed bristles.

However, if you are painting or using Dimensional Magic in conjunction with a Mod Podge project, you will want to use art/detail brushes.

Ruler/Pencil

These will be needed to measure and mark paper or fabric.

Paper Cutter/Scissors

A paper cutter allows you to easily cut accurate shapes and sizes with straight, even edges.

For detailed designs, a pair of sharp craft scissors is recommended.

Straightedge & Craft Knife

If a paper cutter is not available, it is suggested you use a straightedge and craft knife to keep lines straight. *Note: Always remember to protect your work surface with a cutting mat, heavy cardboard or a thick layer of newspapers.*

> ### KEEP IT CLEAN
>
> Speaking as someone who generally embraces the mess of creativity, you've got to know when to clean up.
>
> Mod Podge is a craft that is meant to be fun and messy. For that very reason, it is important to pay attention to how the mess is affecting the project. Take a quick break now and then to clean up the work space—lay down fresh paper, wash your hands well, and then move on. Doing so can help prevent a multitude of sticky mistakes, such as:
>
> - Setting your project in a drip of Mod Podge—on the side that doesn't *need* any.
> - Getting sticky, dirty fingerprints on the wet and tacky Mod Podged paper.
> - Accidentally leaving dried Mod Podge flakes behind on your project and then having to pick them out.
>
> Mod Podge easily washes from fingers, but once it is dried, it will not wash out of clothing. So put on a smock (or your husband's torn shirt that you hate), roll up your sleeves and get out there and make a mess!

Circle Cutter

A circle cutter is the best way to cut precise circles in a variety of sizes with smooth, even edges. They are available in a variety of price ranges and can be as simple as a compass cutter.

Silicone Mat

Covering your work surface is a must. Silicone mats, available at most large craft stores, are wonderfully easy to clean—wait for the Mod Podge to dry and peel it off!

If a silicone mat is not available, use newspaper, butcher paper, old packing paper, a vinyl tablecloth or a drop cloth.

Clear Acrylic Spray Sealer

Apply clear acrylic spray sealer, in either matte or glossy finishes, to completed projects to keep them scratch and dust resistant.

TECHNIQUES & TIPS

Mod Podge is a glue, sealer and finisher all in one bottle. Follow these basic steps for working with paper:

1. Measure and cut paper to size.

2. Use a foam brush to apply Mod Podge to the back of the paper, covering it completely with an even coat that extends to each edge.

APPLICATION

- In most cases, not using enough Mod Podge is a problem more often than using too much. If too little Mod Podge is used, the brayer will push the bubbles down, but there will not be enough adhesive to hold them down.
- It's really hard—not impossible, just really hard—to add Mod Podge after paper is positioned, so it's best to err on the side of "just a bit more."

3. Position the paper, and then press down gently with fingers, starting at one edge and working to the opposite edge, keeping it straight and square as you go. Use one hand to hold the paper up off the project and the other hand to press down gently.

4. Here's where you have—maybe—*one* chance to change it. Since it hasn't been firmly pressed down yet, you should be able to wiggle it a little or peel a portion up if necessary. A word of caution: doing so might lead to rips.

PLAN AHEAD

- Keep a surplus of materials on hand. For instance, buy a little extra of that printed paper. Then if something happens during the project (i.e. it's measured/cut incorrectly, glued askew or wrinkles too badly, etc.) and it has to be pulled off, you have enough of the cherished paper for a second try.

5. Once the paper is in position, use both hands to press it firmly in place, beginning at the center this time and working out to the edges.

6. Use your brayer to smooth out wrinkles or bubbles, again working from the center out.

7. For most of the projects in this book, the Mod Podge process is complete after step 6. Some, however, will include a last step, true to the art of decoupage, in which additional Mod Podge is applied and smoothed over the project. ∎

Baked Ombré Stained Glass

This collection of glass vases stained in graduating shades of the same color gives a stunning ombré effect when showcased as a unit.

Five cylindrical glass vases
of the same size
Gloss-finish Mod Podge®
Clear, gloss acrylic
spray sealer
Liquid food coloring:
blue, red
1 tablespoon water
Craft-dedicated
measuring cup*
Disposable plastic knife
Foil-covered baking sheet
Craft-dedicated cooling
rack*
Glass cleaner
Paper towels
Disposable latex gloves
Oven
*Kitchen items used for
crafting should not be
used for food preparation
afterward.

DIFFICULTY LEVEL

Beginner

TIME TO COMPLETE

Approximately 2 hours (including cooling/drying time)

PROJECT NOTES

Cover work surface and wear latex gloves to protect from food coloring stains.

If you intend to put water in your vases, you need to waterproof them with clear gloss acrylic spray sealer. Consider the shape of the vase to make sure you will be able to spray the interior with sealer.

Vases sealed with acrylic sealer will be water resistant and suitable for displaying fresh-cut flowers. Vases will not be dishwasher safe—hand wash only.

INSTRUCTIONS

1. Cover a baking sheet with aluminum foil. Place cooling rack on foil. Preheat oven to 250 degrees.

2. Make sure vases are clean and free of dust, and that they are not too tall to fit in your oven.

3. Pour six ounces of gloss-finish Mod Podge into measuring cup. Add 1 tablespoon water, 15 drops blue food coloring and 10 drops red food coloring. Mix well with the plastic knife. *Note: If the mixture is too runny, the stain will settle on the glass unevenly and drip to the bottom while baking. If it is too thick, it will settle as goop and refuse to bake clear. Make sure to keep the mixture slightly on the thick side, so you can feel some resistance as you mix.*

4. Pour mixed stain into one vase. Slowly tilt and turn the vase to coat bottom and side surfaces. When all surfaces are coated, turn vase upside down and drain excess Mod Podge back into measuring cup.

5. Place the vase upside down on the cooling rack to continue draining.

6. To the remaining Mod Podge, add 10 drops each of blue and red food coloring; mix well.

7. Repeat steps 4–6 for each remaining vase. Each will be a slightly darker shade of the same color.

8. Use glass cleaner and paper towel to remove stain that may be on the outside of the vase.

9. Remove cooling rack from baking sheet. Place the vases right side up on foil-covered baking sheet.

10. Bake one hour until vases appear transparent. If opaque spots are visible, bake a short time longer. *Note: A white opaque color at the bottom of the vase is normal. When cooled, this will turn a darker shade of the color of the glass.*

11. Remove vases from the oven and let them cool completely.

Tip: If a few hardened spots remain on the outside of the vases, spray with glass cleaner, let sit for a few minutes and scrub off with a sponge or paper towel. Be careful not to get glass cleaner inside the vases.

12. Spray the inside of the vases with clear, glossy acrylic spray sealer. Let dry. ∎

ADDITIONAL IDEAS

You can stain just about anything that's glass! Use this method to achieve a variety of looks:

- Upcycle old vases and different-size jars by staining them the same color and grouping them together as a focal point.

- Try turning an old picture frame into a tray. All you need is paper to cover the inside back of the frame, paint, and some cabinetry handles. Use different colors in the same family—red, orange and yellow, for instance—and drip them over the glass, tipping it in different directions and letting it run over the whole surface. Add some drops of straight food coloring and allow it to drip down for a marbled effect.

- This lamp was created by staining two different-size clear ribbed globes from the lighting department of a hardware store with different orange colors. Holes were drilled in the top of each one with a special glass-cutting drill bit to accept a lamp kit. They were then placed on a base made from a wooden plaque.

Rose Topiary

Create this lovely rose topiary from tissue paper and Mod Podge!
The rolled roses are easy to make in a variety of colors.

DIFFICULTY LEVEL
Intermediate

TIME TO COMPLETE
2 hours, plus drying time

PROJECT NOTES
Cover work surface with silicone mat or other protective covering.

If using craft knife and straightedge to cut strips, use cutting mat, heavy cardboard or thick layer of newspapers to protect work surface.

ROSES
Use paper cutter, or craft knife and straightedge, to cut a total of 60 (3-inch-wide) and 12 (2-inch-wide) strips from both the light pink and dark pink tissue paper.

Medium roses
1. Open one 3-inch-wide strip and place on covered work space. Using a foam brush, blot five spots of Mod Podge evenly spaced across the length of the strip.

2. Place a second 3-inch-wide strip on top of the first and press together flat. Fold this strip in half along the length, making the strip 1½ inches wide. With foam brush, coat both exposed sides of the strip with mod podge.

3. Beginning at one end, roll the strip tightly several times to form the center of the rosette.

4. To begin forming the petals of the rose, holding the center, twist the strip over and press onto the lower section of the center.

5. Turn the rosette a quarter turn and twist and press the strip again.

6. Continue to rotate, twist and press until you reach the end of the strip. Tuck the end under the bottom of the rosette and secure it with Mod Podge.

8. Repeat this process with 3-inch-wide strips to make several medium roses.

9. Let dry overnight.

Large roses
To make several large roses, follow the same process, wrapping to the end of the strip. Then use Mod Podge to attach a second prepared 3-inch-wide strip to the end of the first, and continue to wrap to the end.

Rosebuds
Follow the same process using the 2-inch-wide strips to make 12 rosebuds.

TOPIARY
1. On the wooden dowel, make a pencil mark 3¼ inches from one end and 2¼ inches from the other end. Press the dowel into the 4½-inch plastic foam ball up to the 3¼-inch mark. Remove the dowel and set aside.

2. Working with one rose at a time and arranging light and dark roses in a pleasing pattern, apply hot-glue to the bottom of a large or medium rose and then adhere to the 4½-inch plastic foam ball to cover the ball. *Note: Avoid covering the hole for the wooden dowel.*

3. Fill in gaps between roses with rosebuds so ball is tightly covered. Let dry. Spray covered ball with clear gloss acrylic sealer and let dry.

MATERIALS
- Tissue paper: 11 (20 x 20-inch) sheets each light pink and dark pink
- Styrofoam® brand plastic foam balls: 4½-inch, 2¼-inch
- Terra-cotta pot 3¼ inches wide at top x 3 inches tall
- 12-inch-length 5⁄16-inch wooden dowel
- Green baker's twine
- Small faux pearls
- Gloss-finish Mod Podge®
- Plaid acrylic craft paint: titanium white, baby pink
- Clear, gloss spray acrylic sealer
- Paper cutter, or craft knife and straightedge
- Silicone mat or other protective covering
- Cutting mat (optional)
- Foam brushes
- Round foam paintbrush
- Hot-glue gun

These little rosettes can be used for a variety of different projects!

- To make a wreath, simply follow steps to make rosettes and hot-glue them to a plastic foam wreath form that has been wrapped with matching ribbon. Place roses on front and sides only. Create bow or hanger with additional ribbon.

- For a simple greeting card, hot-glue green ribbon or rickrack for stems and add the rosettes on top. Stamp or write your message on the inside of the card.

4. Paint the inside and outside of the terra cotta pot with multiple coats of titanium white acrylic paint. Let dry. Dip round foam paintbrush in baby pink acrylic paint and press onto outside of pot to make polka dots. Let dry.

5. Spray pot with clear, gloss acrylic sealer. Set aside to dry.

6. Cut a 24-inch length of green baker's twine. Use hot glue to attach one end of the baker's twine to the wooden dowel at the 2¼-inch mark. Tightly wind the baker's twine around the dowel to the 3¼-inch mark. Secure with hot glue. Trim excess twine.

7. Put hot glue on the 2½-inch plastic foam ball and push it, glue side down, into the bottom of the terra cotta pot. Let dry.

8. Push the wooden dowel into the center of the 2½-inch plastic foam ball to the 2¼-inch pencil mark, making sure to keep it straight. Remove dowel and apply hot glue, then reinsert into ball.

9. Apply hot glue to top of dowel, then insert dowel into hole on the rosette ball.

10. Spread hot glue over the top of the plastic foam ball in the pot and then cover with faux pearls, pressing them down firmly to cover the ball. ■

It's a Hoot Magazine Box

Jazz up a generic magazine file box with a little paint and scrapbook paper. This woodland-themed magazine box can hold anything from your kid's school papers to mail.

MATERIALS

Wooden or cardboard
    magazine file box
Patterned papers to
    coordinate with
    acrylic paints
Matte-finish Mod Podge®
Plaid acrylic craft paint:
    light lavender, yellow
    citron, titanium white
Clear, matte spray acrylic
    sealer (optional)
Paper cutter, or craft knife
    and straightedge
Circle cutter
Silicone mat or other
    protective covering
Cutting mat (optional)
¼-inch hole punch
Black fine-tip
    permanent marker
Foam brushes
Detail artist's paintbrush

DIFFICULTY LEVEL

Easy

TIME TO COMPLETE

40 minutes, including drying time

PROJECT NOTES

Refer to Techniques & Tips in General Instructions (page 4) throughout, using photo as a guide for placement.

Cover work surface with silicone mat or other protective covering.

If using craft knife and straightedge to cut strips, use cutting mat, heavy cardboard or thick layer of newspapers to protect work surface.

If using cardboard magazine file box, fill box to support the file sides when applying shapes.

- Use wrapping paper or scrapbook paper to cover the entire surface of the box. Make sure the paper is adhered completely to the box to avoid air bubbles.

1. Use foam brushes to paint magazine file box with acrylic craft paint: light lavender outside, yellow citron inside and titanium white edges. Let dry completely.

2. Use paper cutter, or craft knife and straightedge, to cut tree trunks from patterned papers: For sides you will need two each ½ x 3⅞-inch Tree Trunk No. 1 rectangles, 1 x 5¾-inch Tree Trunk No. 2 rectangles and 1½ x 7¾-inch Tree Trunk No. 3 rectangles. For the back, cut one 2¼ x 8⅝-inch Tree Trunk No. 4 rectangle.

3. Use circle cutter to cut tree tops from patterned papers: For sides you will need two 3¼-inch Tree Top No. 1 circles, two 3¾-inch Tree Top No. 2 circles and two 4⅝-inch Tree Top No. 3 circles. Use circle cutter to cut 11–12 circles varying in size from approximately 1 inch to 2¾ inches for Tree Top No. 4.

4. Mark location of circle cutout on back of box on Tree Trunk No. 4. Cut out with circle cutter or scissors. ***Note:*** *If box does not have this hole, go on to the next step.*

5. Use Mod Podge to adhere tree trunks to box; adhere tree tops No. 1, No. 2 and No. 3 to corresponding trunks. Layer Tree Top No. 4 circles on tree trunk No. 4, overlapping in a pleasing pattern. Let dry.

6. For owl, use circle cutter to cut two 1½-inch circles and one 1-inch circle. Mod Podge one 1½-inch circle to one side of box front for owl body. Cut second 1½-inch circle in half for wings. Mod Podge wings on sides of body. Mod Podge 1-inch circle at top of body, over tops of wings, for head.

7. Use ¼-inch hole punch to punch two circles for eyes; Mod Podge to head. Cut two small triangle shapes for ears, one small triangle shape for beak and two more triangle shapes for feet. Mod Podge in place. Let dry completely.

8. Cut and assemble another owl in the same manner using slightly smaller circles, and adhere on opposite side of box front. Make a third, smaller owl for the box back, placing him above the cutout hole, if there is one.

9. With white acrylic paint and detail artist's paintbrush, paint a white dot or circle in the center of each owl eye; let dry. Use black fine-tip permanent marker to dot pupils in the centers of eyes.

10. If boxes will get heavy use, protect by brushing matte-finish Mod Podge over the entire surface of the box and allowing it to dry overnight. If the boxes will be used primarily for display, finish by spraying surface evenly with clear, matte acrylic sealer instead. ∎

Photo Cube

This cute little wooden cube is an excellent way to display family photos. Match the block to a room's decor, add rub-ons or print words from your computer and you've got a completely personalized photo holder!

DIFFICULTY LEVEL
Intermediate

TIME TO COMPLETE
1 hour, plus drying time

PROJECT NOTES
Cover work surface with silicone mat or other protective covering.

If using craft knife and straightedge to cut strips, use cutting mat, heavy cardboard or thick layer of newspapers to protect work surface.

The model project was made using a computer-generated sentiment. Other options are to hand-print a sentiment or use a stamped or rub-on sentiment.

INSTRUCTIONS

1. Paint all sides of the block with acrylic craft paint. Let dry.

2. Cut five 3-inch squares from coordinating patterned paper. Referring to Techniques & Tips in General Instructions on page 4, use matte-finish Mod Podge to adhere each square to one side of the painted block, leaving bottom blank. Use brayer to remove bubbles. Let dry.

3. Use a computer to generate a sentiment on patterned paper, or use one of the options mentioned in Project Notes. ***Note:*** *Make sure the sentiment will fit within a 2⅞-inch-wide by 2¼-inch-high rectangle.*

4. Cut around sentiment and adhere to front of cube with matte-finish Mod Podge. Use brayer to remove bubbles. Let dry.

5. Measure and mark the center top of the cube. Drill a hole the size of your wire at this mark, drilling at least 2½ inches into the cube. Remove dust.

6. Apply matte-finish Mod Podge to five sides of the cube. Use the angled edge of the squeegee to remove excess Mod Podge. Insert a toothpick into the drilled hole to remove Mod Podge before it dries. Allow the Mod Podge to dry completely.

7. To make the photo holder, cut a 15-inch length of 18-gauge wire. Insert wire in hole in block and mark the wire at the top of the block. Remove wire.

8. At the halfway point between the mark and the far end of the wire, bend at a right angle. Hold wire with bend toward you. Lay a glue stick on top of the bent wire right above the bend. Wrap the wire around the glue stick twice, and then remove glue stick.

MATERIALS

3½-inch wooden cube

Coordinating patterned papers

Craft wire: 18-gauge silver, 28-gauge desired color

Matte-finish Mod Podge®

Plaid acrylic craft paint in dove gray

Clear, matte acrylic spray sealer

Paper cutter, or craft knife and straightedge

Silicone mat or other protective covering

Cutting mat (optional)

Craft squeegee

Toothpick

Glue stick or similarly shaped object

Needle-nose pliers

Drill with small bit

Foam brush

Industrial strength craft cement

Computer with printer (optional)

LIVE LOVE LAUGH

ADDITIONAL IDEAS

For a different twist on this project, use a circular plaque to create a sunburst wreath of photos!

- Paint the plaque in desired color. Mark eight points equally spaced around the edge of the plaque. Drill a small hole an inch or two deep at each mark. Cut and shape eight wire holders of varying lengths and glue into the holes, then decorate the center with decoupaged paper circles and a pretty flower.

9. Push the wire loops tightly together. Use needle-nose pliers to twist the very tip of the wire up and around into a curl.

10. Cut approximately 36 inches of 28-gauge wire. Hold the end of it against the 18-gauge silver wire just over the mark you made earlier. Twist the 28-gauge wire tightly around the straight part of the silver wire, closely covering it all the way to the curl.

11. Trim end of 28-gauge wire and use needle-nose pliers to squeeze the end tightly against the silver wire.

12. Put a small amount of industrial strength craft cement on the wrapped end of the wire holder and push into the hole in the cube. Wipe off excess glue. Let dry.

13. Spray everything with clear, matte acrylic sealer. Let dry. ■

Gadget Charging Station

Turn an inexpensive desktop organizer on its back to create an electronic charging station.

MATERIALS

Desktop organizer with
multiple sections
12 x12-inch coordinating
patterned papers
Washi tape
Mod Podge® Hard Coat
Matte-finish Mod Podge®
Paper cutter, or craft knife
and straightedge
Silicone mat or other
protective covering
Cutting mat (optional)
Drill with 1-inch-hole saw
bit
Sheet of 600-grit
sandpaper (optional)
#0000 steel wool
(optional)
Foam brush

DIFFICULTY LEVEL
Intermediate

TIME TO COMPLETE
2 hours, including drying time

PROJECT NOTES

Place desktop organizer on its back so dividers become shelves. Orientation of organizer in instructions (top, end, back, etc.) refer to this position.

Cover work surface with silicone mat or other protective covering.

If using craft knife and straightedge to cut strips, use cutting mat, heavy cardboard or thick layer of newspapers to protect work surface.

If cutting several similar shapes and sizes, lightly mark each shape's position as you cut it for easier placement.

INSTRUCTIONS

1. Fold 12 x 12-inch sheet of patterned paper in half with the wrong side facing out. Place the organizer on one end on the paper and then trace around it. Use paper cutter, or craft knife and straightedge, to cut paper ⅛ inch smaller on each side, cutting through both layers to make one piece for each end. Set aside.

2. Using single sheets of coordinating patterned papers, trace top and bottom of organizer. Cut out ⅛ inch inside traced lines. Set aside.

3. Measure the dividers (now the shelves) in the organizer and cut paper to fit the top surface of each one.

4. To add interest, cut random strips of patterned paper scraps and adhere to shelf papers with matte-finish Mod Podge.

5. To adhere papers to the organizer, apply a coat of Mod Podge Hard Coat to the wrong side of one piece of paper and position on organizer so it is centered. Referring to Techniques & Tips in General Instructions (page 4), press paper down firmly and use the brayer to eliminate bubbles. Repeat for each surface.

6. Let dry completely.

7. Using drill with hole saw bit attached, drill a 1-inch hole through the back of the organizer, centered in each shelf.

8. To reinforce the holes, cut several 1-inch pieces of Washi tape. Wrap length of tape over edge of hole and press in place. Repeat around the entire edge of each hole (Fig. 1).

Fig. 1

9. Apply Mod Podge Hard Coat over the entire organizer, inside and out. Let dry 15 minutes. Apply a second coat and let dry.

OPTIONAL FINISHING TECHNIQUE

For a thicker, more enamel-like finish, continue as follows:

10. Cut the sheet of 600-grit sandpaper into four equal pieces. Fold one piece in half, dip into water and shake off excess. Wet-sand the entire surface lightly, keeping the sandpaper wet but not dripping. Wipe dry, and then buff with #0000 steel wool.

11. Apply a third coat of Mod Podge Hard Coat and let dry 15 minutes, and then wet-sand as in step 10.

12. Repeat this process until five coats of Mod Podge Hard Coat have been applied and sanded. ■

Antique Photo Tile

Transfer a digital photo to a ceramic tile to create a one-of-a-kind accent piece. Or make several smaller, coordinating tiles to give as coasters. Mod Podge makes it possible.

MATERIALS

6 x 6-inch beige stone or
    ceramic tile

Digital photo

Sheet of white tissue
    paper

Sheet of printer-
    compatible cardstock

5¾ x 5¾-inch square of
    craft felt

Mod Podge® Antique
    Matte

Clear, matte spray acrylic
    sealer

Scissors

Silicone mat or other
    protective covering

Foam brush

Glue stick

Hot-glue gun

Inkjet printer

DIFFICULTY LEVEL

Intermediate

TIME TO COMPLETE

45 minutes, plus drying time

PROJECT NOTE

Cover work surface with silicone mat or other protective covering.

INSTRUCTIONS

1. Adhere felt square to back of tile using hot glue. Set aside.

2. Apply glue stick around just the edges of a piece of printer-compatible cardstock. Unfold white tissue paper, smoothing out the folds with your hands. Press the glued cardstock to the tissue paper. Trim the tissue paper to the size of the cardstock.

3. Size the digital photo to fit onto the tile. Print the picture onto the tissue-paper side of the cardstock.

4. Carefully peel the tissue paper from the cardstock, using scissors if needed. ***Note:*** *Don't worry if it tears a bit or the edges are torn, wrinkled or shabby looking. This will add to the antique appearance.*

5. Fold the edges of the tissue paper so the photo fits well on the tile, and then tear along the folds.

6. Use a foam brush to apply a layer of Mod Podge Antique Matte onto the tile. Center the tissue-paper photo over the tile and begin to adhere starting in one corner. Work your way across the tile diagonally, smoothing out obvious wrinkles or bubbles as you go. ***Note:*** *There will be wrinkles. This is why we used tissue paper—not only does it become nearly invisible on the tile, it also wrinkles nicely when Mod Podged, giving it an aged look.*

7. Continue smoothing the tissue paper onto the tile with your fingers, pressing firmly. Let dry.

8. Apply a coat of Mod Podge Antique Matte over the top. Allow this to dry for at least 15 minutes. Apply a second and third layer, letting dry after each coat. Additional coats may be added to achieve your desired look.

9. Spray the tile with clear, matte acrylic sealer. ∎

ADDITIONAL IDEAS

Use smaller ceramic tiles for coasters!

• Print vintage images in a series—like these antique maps. Stack them together on a coffee table, or bundle them with twine for a great gift.

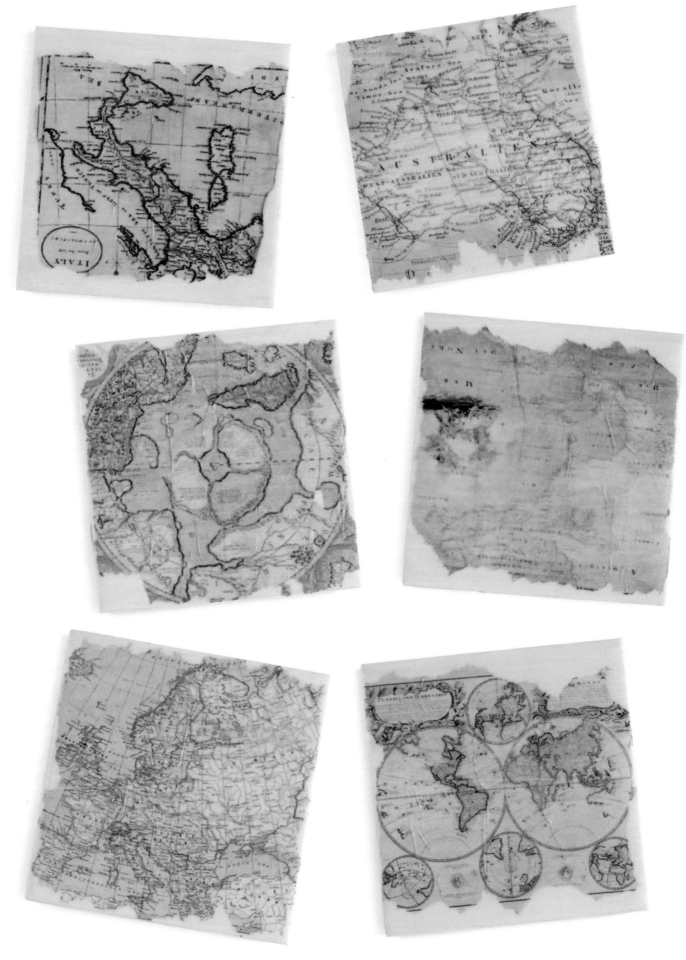

Wiggly Wall Art

Spend some time with the kids or grandkids making something just for them. It's funky and modern—plus, they're sure to love getting messy with you!

DIFFICULTY LEVEL

Easy

TIME TO COMPLETE

1½ hours, including baking and drying time

PROJECT NOTES

Cover work surface with silicone mat or other protective covering.

No worries. Specially made with kids in mind, Mod Podge Wash Out—as the name implies—will wash out of clothing.

INSTRUCTIONS

1. Preheat oven to 250 degrees. Line a large baking sheet or oven-safe cutting board with a 15 x 15-inch piece of baking parchment paper. Use the size and shape of the parchment as a template for the design.

2. Pour some Mod Podge Wash Out into the plastic container. Place a long length of multicolored yarn in the Mod Podge to completely cover. Pull out a yarn end with one hand, and with the other hand lightly squeegee the extra Mod Podge off the string and back into the container. Try to keep the remaining yarn from becoming tangled.

3. Beginning in one corner of the parchment paper, drape the yarn in a scribble pattern, working back and forth across the paper in horizontal stripes to create random loops and waves.

4. Repeat steps 2 and 3 to completely cover the square horizontally, then use the same process to cover the square vertically.

5. When finished covering the square, look for large holes in the pattern—any spots where the yarn looks particular scanty. Fill these by cutting a long piece of yarn, covering it in Mod Podge and laying it randomly over each area.

6. When the area is sufficiently covered, continue to build up yarn layers, this time in completely random patterns—draping, twisting and looping yarn anywhere and everywhere—to fill in the square. Complete five layers of yarn to make the project strong.

7. Cut two pieces of solid-color yarn each approximately two yards long; fold each strand in half, then in half again, to make two four-strand pieces. Hold both pieces together and completely cover the eight strands with Mod Podge. Lay strands in the center of the yarn square and shape into child's first initial. **Note:** *Some initials may require more or fewer and longer or shorter lengths of yarn.*

8. Place the baking sheet in the oven and bake for 30–45 minutes. The yarn will become slightly shiny and hard, but will still be pliable.

9. Remove from oven and allow yarn to cool completely. Peel yarn carefully from parchment. Although still somewhat pliable, the finished piece will be suitable for hanging on the wall of your child's room. ■

MATERIALS

Yarn: small skein multicolored, 4–6 yards contrasting solid-color
Mod Podge® Wash Out
Baking parchment paper
Large baking sheet or oven-safe cutting board
Craft-dedicated plastic container*
Scissors
Silicone mat or other protective covering
Oven
Kitchen items used for crafting should not be used for food preparation afterward.

You can get really creative with this idea!

- Spell out words with the yarn instead of using initials, or change the overall shape.

- Try covering a bowl with plastic wrap, and then draping the Mod Podge yarn all over it. You can't put it in the oven, but after a few days of drying, you'll have a fun scribble bowl! Try different sizes and shapes to produce different results.

Little Rembrandt Art Storage Box

When your little artist brings home mountains of artwork and crafts, think before you purge! With this project, the box itself becomes a portfolio for displaying your child's creativity, with plenty of storage inside.

MATERIALS

Large, heavy-duty photo
    storage box
Child's artwork collection*
Matte-finish Mod Podge®
Brayer
Scissors
Silicone mat or other
    protective covering
Foam brush
*Refer to Creative
Collage Tips.

DIFFICULTY LEVEL

Easy

TIME TO COMPLETE

30 minutes, plus drying time

PROJECT NOTES

Cover work surface with silicone mat or other protective covering.
Refer to Techniques & Tips in General Instructions (page 4).

CREATIVE COLLAGE TIPS

- Choose several drawings and paintings to decorate the top of your box
- Artwork on lighter-weight paper will be easier to work with.
- Choose a variety of shapes, colors and subjects.
- You will be cutting artwork apart to make the collage, so don't select any you want to keep intact.

INSTRUCTIONS

1. Use scissors to cut around artwork images; trim abstract artwork into interesting sizes and shapes.

2. Arrange the pieces in a pleasing pattern on the top of the box lid, overlapping and turning the pieces in different directions to create interest.

3. Working with one piece at a time, use a foam brush to spread matte-finish Mod Podge over the back of each piece and position on the lid. Use your fingers to firmly press the piece into place, and then use a brayer to smooth out wrinkles and press out bubbles. ***Note:*** *It may be impossible to get each piece completely smooth. That's OK. The important part is that the artwork is adhered securely to the box.*

4. Continue in this manner to adhere the selected artwork. When all the pieces are in place, apply a coat of matte-finish Mod Podge over the entire top of the lid. Let dry.

5. If desired, add a name label, and then fill the box with the artist's original designs. ∎

ADDITIONAL IDEAS

With the variety of decorative storage boxes available, the possibilities with this technique are nearly endless!

- Paint a kraft paper box with hinges using acrylic paint, and adhere scraps of patterned paper—as well as one-of-a-kind artwork—to add interest (and help reduce your stash).
- Look for vintage suitcases at thrift stores and garage sales and use this technique to create decorative storage for all kinds of items.

Surf & Sand Bracelet

Add whimsy to your spring and summer wardrobes with a charm bracelet made out of cardstock and Dimensional Mod Podge.

MATERIALS

Double-sided cardstock

Matte-finish Mod Podge®

Mod Podge® Dimensional Magic

Silver chain

Silver toggle clasp

Package 5mm silver jump rings

Two 8mm silver jump rings

Tiny hole punch or large needle

Flower-shaped punches ranging in size from approximately ⅜–1¼ inches

Paper cutter, or craft knife and straightedge

Silicone mat or other protective covering

Cutting mat (optional)

Toothpick

Small wire cutters

Small needle-nose pliers

Foam brush

DIFFICULTY LEVEL
Advanced

TIME TO COMPLETE
45 minutes, plus drying time

PROJECT NOTES
Cover work surface with silicone mat or other protective covering.

If using craft knife and straightedge to cut strips, use cutting mat, heavy cardboard or thick layer of newspapers to protect work surface.

INSTRUCTIONS
1. Use paper cutter, or craft knife and straightedge, to cut cardstock into several 3½ x 5-inch strips.
2. Use paper punches to punch different-size flower shapes from cardstock strips.
3. Using matte-finish Mod Podge, layer different sizes and shapes of flowers in random ways. Bend petals slightly to shape. Let dry.
4. Use a tiny hole punch or a large needle to make a small hole on each flower charm.
5. Apply Mod Podge Dimensional Magic to the front of each flower, working slowly to avoid bubbles and to avoid covering the charm hole. *Note: If bubbles occur, use a toothpick to pop them or push them off of the surface.* Let dry overnight.
6. Measure and cut one length of chain to desired size of bracelet, allowing for the added length of the toggle clasp and large jump rings after assembly. Measure and cut four more lengths of chain, making each progressively longer by approximately ¼ inch.
7. Using needle-nose pliers, attach one end of each chain length to a large jump ring, beginning with the shortest length and adding each graduating length in order. *Note: If the chain's links are not large enough to slip over the large jump ring, attach a small jump ring to each length before slipping onto the large jump ring.* Slip one half of the toggle clasp onto the large jump ring, and then close the jump ring.
8. Attach the opposite ends of the chains to the second large jump ring, and then slip the remaining half of the toggle clasp onto the ring before closing the jump ring.
9. Using small jump rings, attach the flower charms to the chains at random intervals, making sure the fronts of all the flowers are facing the same way. ■

ADDITIONAL IDEAS

Make matching earrings!
- Make flower charms similar to those made for the bracelet, and attach to fishhook ear wires with large jump rings. Wear them with the bracelet as a set or separately for a fun, fresh look.

Child's Artwork Necklace

Wear your child's artwork proudly! This cute necklace is a fresh, new way to display your favorite artist's masterpieces!

MATERIALS

Child's artwork

White cardstock

Bottle-cap bezels with
  jump rings:
  1 (1¼-inch), 6 (⅞-inch)

Matte-finish Mod Podge®

Mod Podge® Dimensional
  Magic

Clear, matte spray acrylic
  sealer

Circle cutter or ½-inch and
  1-inch circle punches

Silicone mat or other
  protective covering

Silver chain

Silver jump rings

Silver lobster clasp

Toothpick

Needle-nose pliers

Foam brush

Computer printer/scanner
  with photo-editing
  software

DIFFICULTY LEVEL

Intermediate

TIME TO COMPLETE

20 minutes, plus drying time

PROJECT NOTE

Cover work surface with silicone mat or other protective covering.

INSTRUCTIONS

1. Scan artwork and save as a JPEG. Open JPEG and resize it to fit inside the bottle caps. Adjust contrast as needed to make artwork stand out.

2. Print on white cardstock. Using circle cutter or circle punches, cut six ½-inch circles and one 1-inch circle to fit inside bottle-cap bezels.

3. Spray the printouts with clear, matte acrylic sealer to set the printer ink so it will not run. Let dry.

4. Apply matte-finish Mod Podge to centers of the bottle caps, and then press cardstock circles into the Mod Podge. Smooth it out with your fingers, pressing firmly all around to secure edges so no dimensional magic can seep under them.

5. Squeeze Mod Podge Dimensional Magic into each bottle cap, covering the circle and filling the bezel to the top. Work slowly to avoid bubbles. If bubbles do appear, pop them with a toothpick right away. Let dry overnight.

6. Cut a length of chain 28 inches long. Attach the large bottle-cap bezel at the center of the chain. Attach the smaller bottle-cap bezels evenly spaced on each side of the center bezel.

7. Using needle-nose pliers and jump rings, attach the clasp to the ends of the chain. ■

ADDITIONAL IDEAS

Use this technique to make personalized gifts for family members!

- Mod Podge a drawing of Daddy in a bottle-cap pendant and attach to a key ring for Father's Day.
- Use a larger bezel pendant to include drawings with slightly more detail. Slide it onto a decorative chain as a perfect gift for Grandma.

Fabric Mosaic Table

Adhere colorful fabric scraps to a small metal table to create an attractive focal piece for a protected patio or porch!

MATERIALS

Round metal patio
   or bistro table
   (Approximately 18
   inches in diameter)
Scraps of four different-
   color, lightweight
   woven fabrics
Mod Podge® Outdoor
Matte-finish Mod Podge®
Clear, matte spray acrylic
   sealer
Scissors
Silicone mat or other
   protective covering
Foam brush

DIFFICULTY LEVEL
Advanced

TIME TO COMPLETE
45 minutes, plus drying time

PROJECT NOTE
   To revive a worn finish or change the color of the tabletop, purchase spray primer and paint. Paint tabletop following manufacturer's instructions.
   Cover work surface with silicone mat or other protective covering.

INSTRUCTIONS
   1. Clean tabletop; dry thoroughly. Spray with clear, matte acrylic sealer; let dry.
   2. Using the templates provided, cut eight Large Flower Petals from each of two fabrics for flower center; cut 16 Large Flower Petals from third fabric; cut 16 Small Flower Petals from fourth fabric.
   3. Arrange petals on tabletop, referring to photo for placement. Working with one petal at a time, lift a petal, use foam brush to apply matte-finish Mod Podge to the tabletop beneath it, and then reposition the petal. Press in place firmly with your fingers, smoothing out wrinkles.
   4. When all the petals are in place, apply a generous layer of Mod Podge Outdoor over the top. Let dry. Apply a second coat and let dry. Apply one to three additional coats, as desired, letting dry after each coat. ■

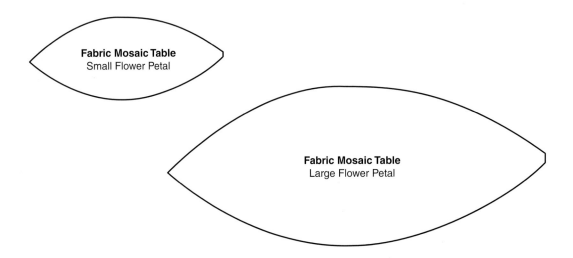

Fabric Mosaic Table
Small Flower Petal

Fabric Mosaic Table
Large Flower Petal

Damask Dresser

Customize a dresser to match any decor! A damask print is a perfect addition to a modern nursery, or even your own updated bedroom.

Wooden dresser with
    smooth-surface
    drawers
Damask-patterned
    wrapping paper
Matte-finish Mod Podge®
Clear, matte spray acrylic
    sealer
Craft knife and
    straightedge
Silicone mat or other
    protective covering
Cutting mat, heavy
    cardboard or thick layer
    of newspapers
Brayer
Toothpick
Foam brush

DIFFICULTY LEVEL

Intermediate

TIME TO COMPLETE

About 2 hours.

PROJECT NOTES

Cover work surface with silicone mat or other protective covering.

When cutting, use cutting mat, heavy cardboard or thick layer of newspapers to protect work surface.

Drawers may vary in size; keep paper with each drawer as it is cut.

The model project was made using a newly purchased dresser, but thrift stores or yard sales often turn up inexpensive pieces that are well suited for a project such as this. To prepare the surface, you may need to scrape off loose paint, fill holes or nicks with wood putty and then apply fresh paint.

INSTRUCTIONS

1. Remove knobs from drawers and make sure dresser is dust free.

2. For each drawer, trace around drawer front onto the wrong side of the wrapping paper. Using a straightedge and craft knife, cut out shape. *(**Note:** If your dresser drawers have a routed edge, measure the area where the paper will be applied.)*

3. Working with one drawer at a time, stand drawer on work surface with front side up. Cover the entire front with an even coat of matte-finish Mod Podge.

4. Referring to Techniques & Tips in General Instructions on page 4, place paper piece on the drawer, starting at one short end, matching edges and making sure the paper is square. Go slowly, gently smoothing small sections and pressing with one hand while the other hand holds the paper away from the surface. Work your way across the entire front of the drawer. *Note: If bubbles or wrinkles occur as you go, gently pull the paper back up and re-apply.*

5. After paper is in position, continue to smooth it more firmly with your hands. Use a brayer to remove bubbles, working from the center out to each edge. Allow the Mod Podge to dry for at least an hour.

6. From the inside of the drawer, insert a toothpick through the screw hole for the knob. Gently press against the paper until you can see or feel the point. Use a craft knife to cut a small X in the paper to allow the screw to pass through the paper without tearing it.

7. Spray the fronts of the drawers and the outside of the dresser with clear, matte acrylic sealer. Let dry completely.

8. Reattach knobs, carefully inserting the screws. ∎

- Mod Podge Hard Coat is a more involved process for furniture, but it will provide a glossy, more enamel-like finish. Carefully follow the instructions on the bottle to apply at least five coats of Hard Coat, wet sanding between coats.

Family Photo Canvases

Create your own family photo canvases to display and brighten any room in your home.

Three color digital family
photos*
Three 8 x 10-inch
stretched canvases
Mod Podge® Photo
Transfer Medium
1–1½-inch-wide lace trim
Spray bottle with water
Staple gun
Foam brush
Inkjet printer
*Refer to Picture
Perfect Tips.

DIFFICULTY LEVEL
Intermediate

TIME TO COMPLETE
Overnight

PICTURE PERFECT TIPS
- Select high-quality images that can be printed at 8 x 10-inch size.
- Since the canvases for this project have a distressed finish, select close-up or near close-up photos.
- Select photos with little or no dominant background.
- The photo will be a mirror image, so if it contains words, mirror the image first when printing.

INSTRUCTIONS
1. Print photos in 8 x 10-inch size. Make color copies of each photo, enlarging 116 percent.

2. Using a foam brush, apply a thick coat of Mod Podge Photo Transfer Medium to the front of one photo, so image is not visible through the medium.

3. Turn photo over and press onto the center of an 8 x 10-inch stretched canvas. Smooth entire surface, pressing down firmly. Smooth edges of paper onto edges of the canvas, overlapping at corners. Allow to dry overnight.

4. Use a spray bottle with water to saturate the surface of the paper until the photo is visible through the paper. Peel off the saturated paper in layers by rubbing with fingertips or a firm sponge. *Note: Rub gently over facial features. If the photo begins to wear away in these areas, stop rubbing. On other parts of the photograph, having the ink pulled away from the canvas can add to the distressed appearance, but care must be taken to prevent this on faces.* Remove paper from sides of canvas in same manner. Let dry.

5. As canvas dries, if you notice paper still remaining in areas, dampen the canvas with a little more water, but do not saturate as before. Use your fingertips to peel off more of the paper. Repeat as needed, taking care not to over-rub. Let dry.

6. Repeat steps 2–5 with remaining two photos.

7. Arrange canvases vertically in the order you wish to display them. Turn canvases facedown with edges even, spacing approximately 2 inches apart. Use a ruler and pencil to measure and mark the center top and bottom edge of each canvas.

8. Cut four 4-inch lengths and one 8-inch length of lace trim. Use a staple gun to attach the end of a 4-inch lace piece to the top edge of the bottom canvas on each side of the center mark. Attach the opposite ends of the same 4-inch lace pieces to the bottom edge of the center canvas in the same manner. Repeat with the remaining two 4-inch pieces of lace to connect the center and top canvases.

9. Staple one end of the 8-inch piece of lace trim to the top edge of the top canvas on one side of the center mark. Staple the opposite end of trim on the other side of center mark to form a loop for hanging. ∎

- Use this technique on any-size canvas. Consider the cost of a large-scale wrapped canvas done professionally—hundreds of dollars! But with just one bottle of Mod Podge Photo Transfer Medium, you can create a black-and-white family photo canvas with ease!
- Have an engineer's print made of your photo at an office supply store. (Some "blueprint" copies lack in quality, but for a distressed canvas this won't be an issue.) Use a bottle of Mod Podge Photo Transfer Medium to transfer the print to a 24 x 30-inch stretched canvas. Finish with Mod Podge Brushstroke in a random crisscross pattern to give the illusion of a painted canvas. Easily frame the piece with Washi tape, or leave as is and paint the edges of the canvas.

Additional Resources

Mod Podge Rocks Facebook Fan Page:
http://www.facebook.com/modpodgerocks

YouTube Instructional Videos:
http//www.youtube.com/modpodgerocks

Plaid Enterprises:
http//www.plaidonline.com

Sources

Mod Podge®, acrylic paint, brayer, silicon mat, mini spouncers and squeegee provided by Plaid Enterprises, Inc.

Mod Podge® is a registered trademark of Plaid Enterprises, Inc. Norcross, Ga., USA. All rights reserved.

 *Modern Mod Podge* is published by Annie's, 306 East Parr Road, Berne, IN 46711. Printed in USA. Copyright © 2012 Annie's. All rights reserved. This publication may not be reproduced in part or in whole without written permission from the publisher.

RETAIL STORES: If you would like to carry this pattern book or any other Annie's publication, visit AnniesWSL.com

Every effort has been made to ensure that the instructions in this pattern book are complete and accurate. We cannot, however, take responsibility for human error, typographical mistakes or variations in individual work. Please visit AnniesCustomerCare.com to check for pattern updates.

ISBN: 978-1-59635-555-2

1 2 3 4 5 6 7 8 9